THE DRAMA LIBRARY

THE MAKERS OF VIOLENCE

By the Same Author

THE STORY OF PSYCHE (A Narrative Poem) *Cambridge University Press*

WENTWORTH PLACE (Poems) *Heinemann*

THE
MAKERS OF VIOLENCE

A Play in Two Acts

BY

ROBERT GITTINGS

WILLIAM HEINEMANN LTD
LONDON

First Published, 1951

Published by William Heinemann Ltd.
99 Great Russell Street, London, W.C.1

Printed in Great Britain by
The Whitefriars Press Ltd., London and Tonbridge

IN AFFECTIONATE FRIENDSHIP

TO GEORGE PHILIP BAKER

Fellow of the Royal Historical Society

UPON WHOSE WORKS

PUBLISHED AND UNPUBLISHED

THIS PLAY IS BASED

The Makers of Violence was commissioned by the Friends of Canterbury Cathedral for the Festival of 1951. It was first produced in the Chapter House on July 18th by John Allen, with scenery by Harald Melvill and costumes by Elizabeth Haffenden. The music for the song was composed by John Hotchkis.

CHARACTERS:

Norse:

OLAF, *a very young man, heir to the throne of Norway.*

RANI, *an old man, hostleader of the Norse troops.*

THRYM, *head of the Norse fightingmen.*

Danish:

CANUTE, *a young man, heir to the throne of Denmark, and leader of the joint expedition against England.*

THORKEL, *known as the Tall, hostleader of the Danish troops.*

HAREK, *head of the Danish fightingmen.*

English:

ALPHEGE, *Archbishop of Canterbury, prisoner in the camp of the Northmen.*

STIGAND, *a monk of Canterbury, his companion, a young man.*

A WOMAN, *wife of the English rebel leader.*

Norse and Danish fightingmen and standard-bearers.

There are two acts. The scene is the camp of the Northmen at Greenwich, and the action is continuous.

ACT ONE

The time is the week after Easter in the year 1012. *The scene is the camp of the Danes and Norsemen at Greenwich, on the bank of the Thames. A high stockade, with a gate right, forms the background. Centre, on a mound, is the double tent of the two princes, made of brightly-striped sailcloth; the raven flag of Denmark is planted on its right, and the Norse lion on its left, each with its standard-bearer. Further right is the single tent of the Danish hostleader,* THORKEL, *on the left that of his Norse counterpart,* RANI. *In front of both these tents are the trestles, benches, stools, drinking horns, flagons, platters and huge bones of old feasts. The flaps of all three tents are shut, and no one is about except the two standard-bearers, who stand motionless; but soon, from the stockade gate, Danish and Norse fightingmen appear, brawling and singing, led by* THRYM *the Norseman and* HAREK *the Dane.*

ALL.

Haro! Haro!
The ox has bled for us!
Our feasting done,
He gives his head for us,
A skull to run with wine like blood,
A marrow bone to crack more food—
Haro! Haro!
The ox has bled for us!

Haro! Haro!
The earth is fed for us,
They fatten fields
To render bread for us,

We wear the wool that others weave,
We glut with gold that others give—
Haro! Haro!
The ox has bled for us!

Haro! Haro!
They live in dread for us,
Their men are slaves,
Their women bed for us,
Our foot is on their kings and priests,
We are the masters, they the beasts—
Haro! Haro!
The ox! The ox has bled for us!

[*The tent-flaps are drawn apart.* RANI *and* THORKEL *appear from their tents, left and right.*]

RANI. Silence!

THORKEL. Silence there, silence!

[*The princes* CANUTE *and* OLAF *are seen playing chess in their tent.*]

CANUTE. Check.

[*A pause while* OLAF *moves.*] And checkmate!

OLAF [*striding down to the men, very angry*].
Who was that bawling and brawling here! Some drunken Dane!

CANUTE [*following*]. Or one of your Norsemen, Olaf?

OLAF [*turning on him*]. One of my men!

CANUTE. Olaf! To lose at chess? So little!

OLAF. But much,
Canute, that every day your Danes contrive
To kill my quiet and murder my men!

CANUTE. Murder!

OLAF. I said Murder!

CANUTE. Now, Olaf—

OLAF. Now, Canute,
Companion and brother-commander!

CANUTE. And fellow chessplayer,
Do not forget!

OLAF. I do not. It is you forget
What we have done, we Norsemen. We invade England,
Break London Bridge, besiege the town, pitch camp
Here at Greenwich, keep this unready kingdom
Trembling in truce. We conquer England, and you,
You drinking-dowsing Danes, you quarrel and murder my Norsemen!
What gratitude!

CANUTE. Gratitude goes as a god disguised,
Often lacking for want of looking. I notice
You set a very high value on your few Norsemen.

OLAF. In every fight my Norsemen have had first place;
We have reaped success, while you—

HAREK [*shouting from the crowd*]. What happened at Canterbury!

DANES [*taking up the cry*]. Yes, what happened at Canterbury!

THRYM [*leaping forward*]. What happened, Harek,
Harek, the Dane? Let Thrym the Norseman tell you.
Harek the Dane was not there!

HAREK. Then let Harek the Dane
Tell Thrym the Norseman this. There were cowards at Canterbury.
Thrym the Norseman *was* there!

THRYM. Prove me a coward then!
Prove it! Prove it!

HAREK. Readily. Now, in this place,
Stand firmfoot, strike freely, then let me strike back if you dare!

THRYM. If you are still there to strike!

HAREK. Easy words! Do!

ALL [*Danes and Norse gathering round*]. Do it, Thrym!

[HAREK *stands ready*. THRYM *lifts his axe, then pauses.*]

THRYM. Here? In the princes' judging-place? Will it be judged
Lawful, my lords?

OLAF. This is fair fight, not murder.

CANUTE. We do not blame heart's blood.

THRYM. Then by the law of heart's blood,
The body and blood of— No! I cannot! I cannot! [*Drops his axe.*]

OLAF. Thrym!

THRYM. I will not strike him!

HAREK. I thought not! And why?
This is the courage you learnt at Canterbury!

DANES [*shouting and jeering*]. Canterbury!

RANI. Princes! Hostleaders! Bone-picking, haunch-biting hench-
men!
Let me tell you, I too was at Canterbury!

THORKEL. No!
How remarkable! The sun may forget to rise,
The moon to set, but Rani the Traveller is everywhere!

RANI. No, not everywhere. Not so near the gallows
As Thorkel the Tall, not by six inches. Did Thorkel
Lead our host to Canterbury? Did Thorkel make
His neck a watchtower to see what happened there? No,
Thorkel stayed here, but Rani was there.

THORKEL. And returned
The better to tell us what happened, no doubt!

RANI. No doubt,
And no doubt what happened.

THORKEL. We know. There was nothing there!

RANI. Then you know wrong. There was a Christ church there.

CANUTE. Was?

RANI. We burnt it. No loss! I have seen better—
Beyond the serpent straits and the peacock sea,
The giant's chessboard glimmering white as narwhale,
Black as basalt, the marble of Rome. We did not
Find that at Canterbury.

THORKEL. No?

RANI. No, Thorkel. Nor where
The east lets down its rosy sails, and eyesight
No longer feels the iceberg strain, but sees
Instead, above the golden bridge, the domes
Of glass, the glass coated with gold, the pale
Long bearded faces bowed beneath wedges of gold—
The floating domes, the rose, the golden city
Constantinople, that once these eyes have known,
I, Rani, the Traveller—well, we did not
Find that at Canterbury!

CANUTE. No indeed. One gilt cross
And some silver goblets as thin as skeleton leaves!

OLAF. What more could we find? We gutted that Christ church like gulls
Whitening a dead whale.

THRYM. I'll witness to that! Let the Danes
Go stir in the ash themselves if they still disbelieve!

HAREK. And find the courage you left there!

CANUTE. Some still believe
There was treasure there. Some say you Norsemen have kept it.

OLAF. By the hammer of Thor, whoever—

RANI. But Canute is right,
Quite right, Olaf. We have got the treasure.

OLAF. Where?
What treasure! Where is it?

RANI. Where? In the tent of Thrym.

OLAF. Thrym!

THRYM. Now by all the gods a man can name,
Not a coin, not one chink or clink of metal—

RANI Not metal
But men.

CANUTE. Men?

RANI. The men we brought from Canterbury.

[*The Danish leaders are amused by this.*]

CANUTE. What! That strange little Christ man and his companion!

THORKEL. The one who was so sick when we sailed from Sandwich!

HAREK. That little round egg-skull just ready for someone to crack it!

RANI. The Archbishop! You laugh? In Constantinople or Rome
You would be laughed at. Patriarch, Pope, Archbishop—
These are like rulers and princes among the Christ men.
They value them.

CANUTE. I see. You mean that—

RANI. I mean
This Archbishop may not be strong like Harek,
Nor half the height of Thorkel, nor wear a king's mantle
As you do, Canute, but to these English Christ worshippers
He is worth royal ransom, and that we shall get for him.
That is the treasure we fetched you from Canterbury! I say—

CANUTE. What was that noise?

OLAF. Some sound in the air!

THORKEL. A swan's
Pinions passing above us?

HAREK [*suddenly pointing*]. Look! Look! Look there!

[OLAF'S *standard-bearer collapses and rolls down the slope.*]

OLAF. My standard-bearer!

CANUTE. Dead.

OLAF. How?

THORKEL. This arrow.

RANI. Let me see.

OLAF. An arrow!

CANUTE. Shot over our heads.

OLAF. An arrow!

CANUTE. A death drop
Out of clear sky.

THORKEL. It came from outside the stockade.

OLAF. Another drunken trick, another murder, a—

CANUTE. Olaf!

OLAF. A Danish joke again! But this time—

RANI. But not a Danish arrow.

OLAF. What's that?

RANI. An English one.

CANUTE. English!

RANI. Its feathers were fledged on an English goose.
It bears a message in English.

THORKEL. Addressed to the man
It shot, no doubt.

RANI. Addressed to the Danish leader.
Read this, Canute!

CANUTE. So! [*reading*] " To the Danes and Norsemen
Camped on our land near Greenwich. We have kept truce
While you have broken it. You have havocked and burnt
Canterbury, and hold our Archbishop captive.
A barge from the Bishop of London waits off the wharf
Bearing what ransom you will. Only release him

First. If he remain a prisoner, be sure
The wrath from heaven will fall on you all."

OLAF. Who says this?

CANUTE. " One Englishman speaking for all the English."

HAREK. The wrath
From heaven!

CANUTE. That means more arrows! Scour the heath,
The marsh and the river margin! A bag of gold
To the man who brings the right hand of this English rebel!

[*Exeunt* HAREK *and the Danish fightingmen.*]

OLAF. My standard-bearer! Another man! Another man!

CANUTE. Let the Norsemen bury their standard-bearer.

[*Exeunt the Norse fightingmen with the body.*]

Come, Olaf,
It seems that Rani was right. They value these Christ men.
Let him be brought here.

OLAF. Thrym, he lodges with you.
Fetch him here.

THRYM. And the other one with him, the young one?

CANUTE. Yes, bring the monk Stigand. He is in the business.
He can tell us the market-price for Alphege.

[*Exit* THRYM.]

RANI These Christ men
Have some sort of saga or legend that one of their lords
In some market fetched only thirty silver pieces.

THORKEL. Thirty pieces! We must do better than that.

CANUTE. We shall. If he is reckoned as you affirm,
His ransom will put money in your pocket,
Which our joint expedition will value. Come, Olaf,
Take my hand and believe in Danish friendship.
There is no need for these differences between us.
My tongue and your temper! Forget them both!

OLAF. I am sorry.
Anger in me is like a fire at sea,
A danger to the whole ship. I am very sorry.
I was angry losing at chess. Let me play you again.
Let me show you I can play without losing my temper!

CANUTE. Play me now, while we wait.

[*Going into their tent.*]

The Archbishop finds,
They say, since he went in your longship, that the dry land
Dances and bobs up and down like a bear in a fairground.

[*Exeunt* OLAF *and* CANUTE *into their tent. The flaps are drawn.* RANI *and* THORKEL *are left outside Thorkel's tent, drinking.*]

RANI. We should leave England.

THORKEL. Why do you say that, Rani?

RANI. This arrow! It came out of nothing, a land of despair.
We have had the spoiling of England. Now we are beginning
To spoil ourselves, this camp with a quarrel a day.
We should be off. Let the salt wind gut our idleness
Before we become the victims.

THORKEL. Restless as ever,
Rani! Why, here is this kingdom as ripe and ready
As wasp-food.

RANI. Who wants it? Oh yes, I know Canute does.

THORKEL. And does not Olaf?

RANI. Olaf is bound for a kingdom
Beyond the compass of Canute.

THORKEL. Your swans
Have always to be the whitest! Now, why not talk sense?
Norway is only a vassal state of Denmark, and
Your Olaf only an orphan, a pretender to the throne.
He is lucky to share this adventure. If he can touch
A half of this land, I strongly advise him to take it.

RANI. And why do you give this advice?

THORKEL. I think it may help him.

RANI. No. You think two young rulers, dividing and quarrelling,
May leave the mastery of England to Thorkel the Tall!

THORKEL. Well! How you jump down the jaws of suspicion!
Perhaps it is your digestion, now journeys are done.
Come on, take a turn round the ramparts, Rani the Traveller!

RANI. And be a target?

THORKEL. My height will be your healthguard.
And talking of targets, what kingdom does Olaf aim at?

RANI. One that he does not know yet. One that comes not
To those who plot their life as they play a chess-game.
One that I know he was born for, though I cannot bring him
The way to win it. One that his own heart, or
A wiser than I must teach him.

THORKEL. A wiser than you!
Perhaps you mean a wilier?

RANI. Judge by yourself.
Come on now, Thorkel, come on!

[*Exeunt* RANI *and* THORKEL. *Enter* THRYM.]

THRYM [*calling over his shoulder*]. Come on, come on!
Come on!

STIGAND [*off*]. Father Alphege must move carefully!

THRYM. Father Alphege must move carefully, must he!
What about me? Come on now, muscle makes movement!

[HE *and* STIGAND *half-carry* ALPHEGE *and sit him on a bench.*]

ALPHEGE. Thank you, my sons. I owe you thanks indeed,
And in a double and a different measure,
Both to you, my friend, and you who last night
Became my friend.

THRYM. No thanks to me. I tell you
It's no good.

STIGAND. What is no good?

THRYM. What he told me last night.
All I ask is, don't tell them. I've been jeered at,
Cursed at, and called a coward, and that's quite enough.

STIGAND. Blessed are ye when men shall revile you.

THRYM [*with axe*]. Enough,
Whelp! Do you want a tap from skull-splitter here?
It wasn't your whining taught me the Christ words. I did it
For his sake.

ALPHEGE. You have done so much already.
You have taken me into your tent, you have fed me, tended me,
Dressed my wound. I would not have you suffer
More for my sake.

THRYM. How can I help but suffer
If you make me say the Christ words and do the Christ things?

ALPHEGE. Then you suffer for Christ, not me.

THRYM. Then I'll suffer
For Christ no more! It's not that I care what Danes do.
Danes would heave their filth in anyone's face;
But when my master Olaf gives me that eyelook,
Blue and bleak, the ice-blink, then, then I tremble
As winter and arctic whale-chase never once made me.
I'll not feel ashamed in front of him! I've finished
With Christ and kindness and all that love-to-my-neighbour—
And if you dare tell them, this axe will widen your mouth-
piece.
Remember that when you talk! Remember skull-splitter!

ALPHEGE. We shall remember, Thrym, but will you forget?
We shall do as you wish; but you must now do
Even as you now are.

THRYM. Am I so different? Am I
Changed? Am I one bone or fingernail altered?
Ah! You thought I would be! I thought I should be
After that saga of Christ you spun last night.
Not a bit! When I met them this morning, Thrym was Thrym
The Norseman still. I did not love my brother
Harek the Dane. I hated him, hair and hide.
I am not one of your kind, nor you of mine.
I am the same as before, I tell you!

ALPHEGE. You are
A man who argues for and against himself,
For and against his soul and whom it should serve.
That was not so before, and you know it.

THRYM. I know
Your Christ words, and this cross you gave me to wear
Under my collar, risk my neck in this camp!

[*He is fumbling with the cross round his neck, when the flaps of the princes' tent part.* OLAF *and* CANUTE *come out, as* THRYM *hastily thrusts the cross away again.*]

OLAF. Thrym!
Why did you not say the Archbishop was here!

THRYM. I was warning him—

CANUTE. Of what?

THRYM. To show respect and watch what he says.

CANUTE. He knows that already, we hope.

THRYM. I hope he does!

[*The standard-bearers have brought two chairs from the tent.*]

OLAF. Our seats of judgment are set. Call every man
Who has an interest in this to come and attend it!

[*Exeunt standard-bearers.*]

STIGAND. And place a chair for Father Alphege. He is old,
Old and weak.

CANUTE [*sitting*]. We see he is old and weak.

OLAF. Give him a stool.

[THRYM *fetches one.*]

ALPHEGE. Thank you, my son.

THRYM [*touching his axe*]. Remember!

ALPHEGE. I shall remember that you have treated me kindly
However harshly I may be brought to judgment.

CANUTE. Now, Alphege, we are waiting for your attention,
[*to* STIGAND] And yours. We have not brought you here for judgment.

ALPHEGE. Nor could you. I obey no law of yours.

CANUTE. Oh but we could, Alphege. The law of England
Does not run here.

ALPHEGE. The law I obey runs everywhere.
The god of mercy still rules.

CANUTE. No one rules here
Except our joint command. Is that understood?

ALPHEGE. Perhaps; but not by me.

OLAF. This means nothing to us!
Archbishop Alphege, we are here to settle your ransom.
In Canterbury, when you refused to show us
The treasure of your cathedral, we brought you here
For further questioning. We are now persuaded,
Though there may not have been treasure at Canterbury, you
Are worth that treasure to us.

ALPHEGE. I am worth nothing.

CANUTE. But we know better than that. We have had a message
Here from your friends. We know they value you highly.
How highly?

[*Hands* ALPHEGE *the message. He reads, then tears it.*]

ALPHEGE. I am worth nothing, in spite of my friends.
They are confused by love and fear. They use
Words, like children, before they know their meaning,

As indeed they are children, in puzzled despair, in faith.
It is true I love them, and they love me; and yet
I am less than one breath among them, worth no more ransom
Than simple pity would render the poorest his freedom;
But before God, I am told, my value is infinite,
And not to be paid in your coin.

OLAF. I think you are using
Words very strangely. Men are one thing or another,
Worth something or nothing.

CANUTE. And here, in our common judging-place,
Their bodies obey one law, either captive or free.

ALPHEGE. I am both captive and free, though neither to you.
How can you possibly value my body here?
Body at best is only a kind of witchcraft,
A wisp, a delusion, a feeble marshlight that floats
Over the fen of deception that we call life.
Listen; and let me tell you not fable but fact.
When you men from the North first circled Canterbury
I was amazed, such people, the gold-haired sunrise,
The blue-eyed noon, the stature of evening elm-trees,
In aspect like the angels ranking out
To fight their wars in heaven. Or so I thought,
Until that night, that third night, when our cloisters
Spouted scarlet, and black with ember, and white
With ash, and stark with cruelty, your men strode
Howling and hacking hate against God's altar—
And against me, if Stigand here had not saved
All except this arm-thrust—why then, if truly
I had painted devils, I should have drawn them
In your shapes. Yet either would have been wrong, though both
Together were right. For such is the nature of men,

As you, who profess to rule them, princes, should know—
Not one, but two.

[*While* ALPHEGE *speaks*, RANI, THORKEL, HAREK, *and some of the fightingmen have drawn near, and stand listening.*]

THORKEL. Well! What a saga! It seems
We are all starving for want of words. He has swallowed
The lot, like a Lapland sorcerer. The little wizard!
But this is nonsense! There are no angels or devils
Except in the old tales. Men are men, nothing more;
Good fellows, or, at the worst, good animals. Treat them
Well, and they fight; badly, they desert; offer them
Enough, and they will do anything. No angel-devils
But men, whose service it takes a man to command.

ALPHEGE. He who believes that will never come into his kingdom.

CANUTE. What kingdom? Why did he say that, Thorkel?

THORKEL. What kingdom?
Why, I did not speak of kingdoms. I am only a man,
A plain man among men. You all know Thorkel!

RANI. We do!

CANUTE. You are well-known, Thorkel. And you, Archbishop,
What business have you to talk of kingdoms, you who come
Chirruping out of your stonechat cloister, you
Who never commanded the loyalty of a louse?

STIGAND. That is not true! You do not know Father Alphege.

CANUTE. I do not know you.

STIGAND. You will. I am your answer.
You think Father Alphege is weak. Let me witness

How strong he can be. Which of you, at midnight,
When every tussock crimps with frost, and birds
Lump frozen down from branches, would stand barefoot,
Bare-headed, till dawn?—and not like wolves because
The warm hope of the kill kept hot your hearts
On sentry-go; he, being old and unhardy,
Does this merely in duty. But more than that,
I say that he is strong because he commands
The love and not the fear of men; and that
Is why I serve him.

CANUTE. You do him little service
Now, and less to yourself. We shall soon test this.
Harek! Take this raw blackbird by the neck!
Now see what tune he whistles; and will his master
Still sing the same from his obstinate perch, still give
Our law and justice no answer when he sees
His loyal servant gripped? Twist his ear, Harek!
What will you say now?

ALPHEGE. Forgive them. Forgive them, Lord,
For they know not what they do.

STIGAND [*in pain*]. O Lord, forgive them!

CANUTE. This patter! Have his ear off, Harek!

OLAF [*leaping up*]. No!
Stop this! Stop this, I tell you! Let him go!
Let him go, you, Harek! The man is as brave as you.
What, do you not obey! [*Strikes him.*]

HAREK. Order your own men,
Sea-spawn of Norway!

OLAF. You Danish animal! Order
My own men! Thrym, I command—

THRYM. I need no command!
Let the Christ man go! No? Then take that for him,
And that for me too! Oh, what a relief!
I can hit twice as hard now!

HAREK [*releasing* STIGAND *and raising his axe*].
Thrym, you blunderskull, you—

RANI. Stop this brawl! Is this judgment? Is this a court
Or is it a cattle-market? Strike if you like,
But reckon with Rani thereafter. As for you, princes,
Let my advantage of three-to-one in age
Tell you to sit in judgment, not in torture.

ALPHEGE. Nor do they sit in judgment, no; but this
Has judged them, the one from the other.

STIGAND Oh Father, do not
Provoke them, for your own sake. I can stand more,
Much more for you, if you will go safe.

OLAF. This man
Is faithful to you, Archbishop. I think I see why,
Though I myself would not be.

ALPHEGE. It is early yet.

OLAF. I do not know what you mean. I do know this, though.
Rani is right. This may be Danish judgment.
It is not ours.

CANUTE. Rough words ask for rough handling.
Who judges here, these men or we?

THORKEL. Or Rani!

RANI. Experience is a form of judgment. I speak
For experience. You are wrong to undervalue him.

The lord of these Christ men sold for thirty pieces
Of silver; and he is dead. The living are
A hundred times the worth of the dead, in gold
And no less metal. Why not make this man's ransom
Three thousand pieces of gold?

CANUTE. He will not be ransomed.
Did you not hear that?

RANI. I did not hear him asked.
There are ways and ways about it. Now, Archbishop Alphege,
You are bone and flesh of your English people.
Pay us the ransom I have named, and then
Go back to your people. Go back to your proper place.

ALPHEGE. My place is with the people of England. I am,
As you say, their bone and flesh.

CANUTE. And the price is just.

ALPHEGE. What? No! No price is just that pays for souls.
Is that where your suggestion leads? Then surely
It would be blasphemy for me to bargain
And seal the act with ransom. Cannot you see
That man is not a commodity? He pays
No port-due, no excise, to protect the mystery
Of being, the patient industry of mere living,
The ultimate rare manufacture of the soul.
So let me repeat, no ransom! And one matter more—
My proper place! Reason says there, out among
The charred roof-fallen tragedy of my people.
Reason says wisely; but why am I here, if I
Were not intended to be here? No answer
From reason; but I already begin to have answers

Here, in this camp. I tell you, the purpose that sent me
Plainly begins to show, yes, even in the tent
Where you have lodged me, yes, even there among those who—

[THRYM, *who has been watching* ALPHEGE *uneasily throughout, suddenly rushes at him with uplifted axe.*]

THRYM. Silence, or see your brain-pan scattered!

OLAF. Thrym!
What, are you mad as well as the Danes? Must you
Manhandle justice like them?

THRYM. I meant—I was trying—

OLAF. Silence! Get to your tent before I strike you!
Go! Go!

[*Exit* THRYM.]

RANI It seems to me, this open-air judgment
Invites too many droppings of interruption.

THORKEL. What better can you suggest?

RANI. I suggest all
Come to my tent. Let us hear this man in quiet.
That is, if our raven cousins find it agreeable.

CANUTE. We agree, Rani.

[CANUTE *and* OLAF *cross to* RANI'S *tent.*]

RANI. My canvas will be surety
For your safekeeping, Alphege; no cloister-cell
But as good a snail-shell as can be carried around.
You are very welcome to it.

ALPHEGE. I thank you, friend.

[*He follows* CANUTE *and* OLAF *into the tent.*]

RANI. Will you come, Thorkel?

THORKEL. I have some business here.
You will be better without me; and I without you.

[RANI *goes in.* HAREK *pounces on* STIGAND.]

HAREK. Now we can tear him to tatters!

THORKEL. Harek! What!
Harm this Englishman? How can you think of it!

HAREK. You're joking!

THORKEL. Joking! You heard what Olaf said? Have I
To say the same to you? It seems I have!
Get to your tent, carrion! Go, go, you lump of houndsmeat!

[HAREK *withdraws, as* THORKEL *laughs at his discomfiture.*]

Ha, ha! Well, blackbird, no need to gape so beakily.
I know courage, even in your odd disguise.
We have rough rules-of-thumb for it. You have stiff ways
Of trial, or so I hear, within your cloister.
Is that not so as well?

STIGAND. It is as I said.
Father Alphege never spares himself; we cannot
Do less.

THORKEL. Of course not; and you did nobly, splendidly.
Sit down. Drink. No? Right again. Our finest
Feather-splitting, wand-dividing bowmen
Hardly ever touch it. It needs a stronger man [*drinks*]
To restrain than to indulge. Let none deny that!

STIGAND. I am not strong; but I am glad you do not
Despise us after all.

THORKEL Despise you? No.
Why, even to say that proves you are not a weakling
But a man with decent pride, a man—

STIGAND. No, no,
I am not proud, I hope.

THORKEL. I only said
Decent pride. Come now, you are proud of your master?

STIGAND. Indeed yes. All our people are proud of him. I mean
The people of England, not only the monks of Canterbury.

THORKEL. The people of England respect your master?

STIGAND. They would die for him!

THORKEL. Die for a person who does not rule them?

STIGAND. He rules them
More than the king and his council. He rules their hearts.

THORKEL. I see that he rules yours. Well now, but suppose
He stops here in this camp, and rejects all ransom—

STIGAND. Yes, yes, that is what I fear.

THORKEL. You fear; but he
Desires it. I ask you why?

STIGAND. He sees God's hand in it.

THORKEL. But you do not. [STIGAND *is silent.*] I can see something too.
Your master has the wisdom to behave
Just like the cuckoo.

STIGAND. I do not understand. I—

THORKEL. All men who hear the cuckoo go to find it,
Calling, calling, deep among the spear-top pines.

All men who hear that he is in our camp
Will rally to rescue him. So he sojourns here
By choice, the choice of danger, danger for us,
Though it is danger for him too, as you observe.

STIGAND. I do, I do; I wish—

THORKEL. You wish he would not.
I know. I think I can help you. You see this ring?
A lump of amber from the Baltic beach
Set raw in the silver. Many have felt its flail
Across their faces. Why do you flinch? It is
A peace-borrower for you. With this ring, all
Who guard the alley to the river-wharf
Will give you conduct, yes, and will row you out
To where the ransom barge chops tide. If and when
Violence shall make this camp a new volcano,
As may be when the mass of force finds outlet,
Say of revenge for treacherous attack,
Or even some word-blown less-than-rumoured cause—
If that occur, or better, before, remember
This ring. It is on my finger. This is my tent.
I am a friend. One says no more to those
Whose minds are trained to follow.

STIGAND. If I should take
The ring at once!

THORKEL. Then you could bring his ransom
Here in a quarter of an hour—on one condition.

STIGAND. I will take the ring! What is your condition?

THORKEL. This.
If, as I know is your habit, you should write
Chronicles of this occurrence, set it down

Plainly, and to the people of England, that I,
Thorkel, saved their Archbishop. Tell them what sort
Of man I am.

STIGAND. I accept your condition. The ring!

[ALPHEGE *suddenly emerges from* RANI'S *tent.*]

ALPHEGE. My son! My son! I felt you were in danger!

STIGAND [*running to him and kneeling*]. Father! Father!

THORKEL. Well, you know where to find me,
Another time!

[*He goes into his own tent and draws the flaps.*]

ALPHEGE. I blame myself, so set
On what I have to do among this camp,
Among these people, that I left you here
Alone, in cruel hands; but you—?

STIGAND. No one
Has harmed me, father.

ALPHEGE. Thanks be to God. It is
The one-eyed blindness of our obstinacy
To think that what we do, the main mission,
Outweighs all little minor cares and acts
That are the total and true sum of life.
But you are safe. Now go to our tent, to Thrym's.
Yes, go to Thrym. His way is threaded with ours,
However he tangles it. You may do much for him
While he is charging head-down at the blazon
Of new ideas. Yes, that is your place, by the side
Of his difficult conversion.

STIGAND. But what about you?
Why may I not do what every instinct says,

I, elected by violence to stay by your side,
I, of all monks at Canterbury, captive with you,
Why else except every moment to stay with you, serve you,
You, our one hope, our life, and you only!

ALPHEGE. I?
I am a small vein knotted in one of the fingers
Of a great hand; but the hand upholds us all.
Go to your place, my son; I go to mine.

[ALPHEGE *watches* STIGAND *go, and then slowly turns back himself towards* RANI'S *tent.* HAREK *and the fightingmen enter singing snatches of their song. They put the two chairs back in the princes' tent, and depart making gestures of mock threat at* ALPHEGE, *who crosses himself. As* ALPHEGE *turns again to* RANI'S *tent,* CANUTE *suddenly emerges from it, drawing the flaps behind him.*]

CANUTE. Wait! Before you waste words on these Norsemen,
Hear mine!

ALPHEGE. Very well.

CANUTE. I know I am young; but what
It is about you, I am not too young
To know. I know the need to learn; I know
I have the power to learn. Authority
Is a profession like the rest—to be learnt.

ALPHEGE. Why do you say this to me?

CANUTE. Because you have
A secret to teach me.

ALPHEGE. I am not much of a hand
With secrets. Thorkel was wrong to call me a wizard.
I hope you did not believe him.

CANUTE. I only believe
Those things I know and see. I know my father
Is King of Denmark. I know that he will die.
I know I shall be king; but I see further.
You know where Denmark is?

ALPHEGE. I have not travelled there,
But it is not unknown to me.

CANUTE. I am sorry.
I was being over-serious. You did right
To smile at me. Now, if you will, sit down
And listen to my purpose. First, make your mind
A map, a chart of many coasts. See them—
The rock-toothed channels, the soft-mouthed rivers, easy
For town and trade, the great green enemy ice-castles
Locking and bridging, and then the warm underworld stream
That brings fantastic seaweeds on its proffer,
The tributary provinces of an empire, yes,
An empire with its overcoat of land
Ripped inside-out, and sleeved and seamed with wave-threads,
The whale-track and the gannet-line; but where,
Where on this sea-bird's sweep of wing stands Denmark?

ALPHEGE. The salt is on your tongue, my son. It flickers
Like phosphorous over your fingers. Tell me, and I,
No sea-bird, still will try to follow.

CANUTE. It lies
There, there, out on the iron-bound rim of the circle,
Behind the bars and shoals of plume-white danger,
Straitened, remote, a pirate crow's-nest, not
The capital for a king. Now, follow my sea-bird
Home to the solid hub of the ocean wheel.
What is this land that draws all men, whose men

Are not to be drawn from destiny? It is England;
This land; and among this land of Englishmen
I seek out you, Archbishop.

ALPHEGE. I?

CANUTE. You. Of all men,
My sea-bird lights upon your shoulder.

ALPHEGE. Then
He must have mistaken his perch. I am not a sailor,
Oh no, ask the Norsemen. When I went aboard
At Sandwich, they pushed me up a plank as narrow
As the difference between faith and heresy.

CANUTE. And what
Did you do, between the solid faith of land
And the heresy of shifting water?

ALPHEGE. I?
I shut my eyes.

CANUTE. You cannot now. Oh no,
Archbishop, let me finish. Small men go on
As they begin; the great are always growing.
I grow. My project is to rule an empire
Here, from this chosen island. This is the chess-man
To which my chain of moves is anchored, a man
Not ivory, but of his people's bone and flesh.

ALPHEGE. You would say me.

CANUTE. I do say you. You are
The key. Your figure-head king, flitting and edging
From castle into castle, is no leader
For a loam-stubborn land like yours; but you, Archbishop,
Mild-looking, are immovable.

ALPHEGE. What do you want?

CANUTE. Simply this; to make this land of England
The pulse and heart-beat of an empire, and
To have my capital here among Englishmen.

ALPHEGE. And
Do you expect to rule them against their will?

CANUTE. No, with it.

ALPHEGE. Can I believe that? when I have seen
Not half an hour back how one Englishman
Has suffered at your hands?

CANUTE. You know yourself
There must be necessary firmness. He is no worse.

ALPHEGE. He is no worse, but you are.

CANUTE. How is that, then?

ALPHEGE. You are less than you were; and every deed you do
In that dimension will diminish you
Till you are nothing, and your forced rule of England
Lose all respect.

CANUTE. Ah! That is where you help me.

ALPHEGE. I help you?

CANUTE. As I help you. I shall restore you,
Rebuild your churches, keep you as my Archbishop
If you will do as I say when I am king.

ALPHEGE. And what does an Archbishop do when you are king?

CANUTE. He smoothes my way; he acts as intervener.

ALPHEGE. The only intervention known to me

Is that between the struggle of soul with self,
And never between the conqueror and his victims.

CANUTE. Victims? No, but you benefit. Your people
May worship under me.

ALPHEGE. But under you?

CANUTE. There must be one who rules.

ALPHEGE. There is; not you.

CANUTE. Come now, there is no need to steer your words
So close the wind. I shall have kings beneath me,
Norway, Sweden, Iceland, Scotland, Ireland,
All will kneel here and pay allegiance; need you
Consider yourself exempt? You will have more
Real power than any of them.

ALPHEGE. I shall; but not
Derived from you. My son, the answer is No.

CANUTE. I see. No more than that?

ALPHEGE. No more than that.

CANUTE. But why not give your reasons? I have been
Aboveboard. I have advanced my move, my plan.
Now play me yours, and I perhaps will see
Directions to amend, or chance to improve,
And so, by deliberate interweave of black
And white, a kind of pattern is squared out
That could not spring from either. Tell me your reasons.

ALPHEGE. My son, I can tell you nothing; except this;
What you say is temptation, of a kind
Many men would think foolish not to follow.

CANUTE. Why then—

ALPHEGE. But it must not be followed! If
The last death-rattle in a nation's throat
Demanded it, still it could not be followed.
You know what you are seeking for; but I
Know too. It is not for a king who rules
Denying Christ.

CANUTE. That might be come at, too.

ALPHEGE. You cannot come at such a thing with terms
Such as you use. Should I attempt to teach you?
No. If I tried to cloak belief about you,
Your self-sufficiency would shrug it off,
Would shrug me off, just as it took me on.
I cannot teach you.

CANUTE. Why not? What do I lack?

ALPHEGE. You lack that cranny of weakness where the seed
Of wandering faith may lodge and grow.

CANUTE. I am sorry,
Very sorry for both of us. We might
Have had some use for each other. Now perhaps
Mistakes may queer the pitch of both our quests.
A pity.

ALPHEGE. My pity is for you.

CANUTE. I wonder.
Are you still set to stay here, still refuse
Ransom?

ALPHEGE. You see me here.

CANUTE. Talk to the Norsemen,
Then tell me what you think. Olaf has not
My even temper. His passions fork with lightning

And crash with thunder. You will smell sulphur round
Your steeples once again. You may be glad
To walk my way after all.

ALPHEGE. Are you not afraid
I may walk his?

CANUTE. I do not think so. No.
He has no way, except the long voyage round
To being my vassal. He will kneel to me
And pay allegiance sooner or later. I own
Olaf as Denmark owns Norway.

ALPHEGE. God owns both,
And pride owns nothing, Canute.

CANUTE. Remind me of that
When you kneel too! I wonder! If you are plotting
For Olaf and against me, remember I
Am watching. Olaf is my strong arm; but I
Would cut my arm off, however strong, once I
Suspected it would not serve my purpose. And you,
Archbishop, once I suspect you work against me,
I will cut you off too.

ALPHEGE. Is this your even temper,
Canute?

CANUTE. It is the truth. You talk to Olaf.
You will come running to me when the angry hive
Swarms in his head.

[OLAF, *with* RANI, *appears abruptly from* RANI'S *tent.*]

OLAF. What is this? A conspiracy,
Canute? You went to fetch him—

CANUTE. Well, there he is.

ALPHEGE. Yes, I am still here.

CANUTE. Did you think that he
Would plot with me to set him free? Really,
You can have no conception of this Englishman!
He will not pay, he will not go. Before
Your time is out, you will be paying him
For the privilege of having captured him. So much
For the treasure you found at Canterbury! Rani!
I think that we should have a game of chess.
Olaf lours like a cloud-burst. Leave him to break.
Here in my tent I have a set of men
Bought from an Arab expert at the game
Beyond all others. Come in and play me, Rani.

[*Exeunt* CANUTE *and* RANI *into the princes' tent.*]

OLAF. So you will not be ransomed. Do you know
What you are doing?

ALPHEGE. I am doing what seems to be right.

OLAF. You are making me think you have some other motive,
Just as you did at Canterbury when I struck you
Because you would not reveal your treasure. Do
You want me to strike you again?

ALPHEGE. Do you think
That will reveal a treasure, any more
Than when you did it before?

OLAF. I do not know.
It might. It might reveal to me what motive
You have for staying here, refusing ransom,
Acting as if you owned our daily lives,
Or at least as if we did not own them. What

Possible motive can you have for this?
Are you a spy perhaps?

ALPHEGE. Perhaps I am.

OLAF. You are!

ALPHEGE. But not as you suppose. I think
It may be said that I was sent here.

OLAF. Sent!
We hauled you here; that is the only word for it.

ALPHEGE. No, Olaf, there are other words for it;
Words not so much on your lips, but in that heart
You brass about with roughness and disdain.
Yes, you struck me at Canterbury; then what did you do?
You put me in the care of your best man,
Your bodyguard, Thrym, whom you could trust to tend me,
Protect me, and make his tent my sanctuary.
Why did you do that? We have a word for this.
It might be compassion; it might even be repentance.

OLAF. It might be neither; in all common pride
We could not treat you like those cannibal Danes.
That is the only reason.

ALPHEGE. Very well then.
Now, today, in this place, not half an hour back,
Why did you take the part of one who, to you,
Was nothing, only a follower of mine,
Less than the least distinguished? Was this pride
Before the Danes, to rescue him, come down
From your high seat of judgment, and descend
To pity? Yes, pity! And I still would use
That word although you struck it from my mouth!

OLAF. It seems to me you try to hide your motives
By holding mine up for flattery. Nothing of the sort!
I tell you, it is simply this. I cannot
Endure the oppression of any person who
Trusts in fair dealing and is cheated of it.
You know how it was with me in my own country?

ALPHEGE. I had heard some rumours.

OLAF. Nothing so bad as the truth.
It is a wrong from birth. My father was
The rightful king of Norway, no dispute
However the Danes might sulk across the straits.
We were at peace then; he was a simple man,
Too simple. He rode the boundaries of our land,
Ate fish and milk one day, and flesh and ale
The other like a peasant, simply dressed
And friendly with all his subjects; often away
From home, my mother, by then carrying me,
Must have thought, and unthought, until that day
When the news came, the same that I was born.

ALPHEGE. What news, my son?

OLAF. That he was dead; and dead
In such a way; in the house of a foreign woman,
Burnt to death, decoyed there by the Danes.
I do not blame him, only them. My mother
Was firm on that, and Rani—for when he
Hid us, while Denmark like a friendly wolf
Suckled our orphan country, I was cradled
In one idea, to win our land again,
My stolen birthday gift. Very well then.
Now the second betrayal. It could not be winked at
Whose son I was, when Rani brought me out

Trained beyond common endurance—when I had swum
The ravening ice-jawed water that divides
The Baltic from the Northern Ocean, and shook
My shoulders broadly on the Danish shore.
What to do with me, that was the question. And when,
By Rani's advice, I offered to lend an arm
And a small legion of strength from our own land,
A following grown up with me, to reinforce
Their expedition to England, they could not refuse
With any pretence of truth; but they could and did
Cheat me again!

ALPHEGE. You do not seem to me
A man easily cheated.

OLAF. Nor am I! And if
I should construe that quiet tone as shielding
A liberty to laugh, I had better warn you,
As you should know, I will not bear that long!
I took the Danes for as good or bad as their word,
This project here a path to fit myself
With a picked and fighting army, and provide
Out of the plunder of England golden bars
To slot the ladder leading to the throne—
Money to pay my men, all men like me
Looted out of their homelands and good country
By Danish overseers: then with that money
To turn my back, as Rani says, and leave
This rawly-beaten island, and return
And take my own land. But we are cheated! They
Keep from our winnings all but our common pay,
Yes, and in countless accidental actions,
See my men killed. And you stand smiling there
As if all this disappointment were nothing!

ALPHEGE. Nothing
Is ever entirely nothing. If I did smile,
It was not at your misfortune, but to see
The mixed malleable compound of man; how he
Can be so wise for others, and so wrong
When he confronts himself. How he knots up
A net of every action but the truth
To capture his desire. How he deceives
No one except himself, yet every day
Repeats the flimsy reason to his deafness,
And will not hear another voice.

OLAF. Do I
Deceive myself then? I do not. My life
Is plain to me. It should be clear to you,
All that I need is money, to reward
My faithful men and take my rightful kingdom.
Your ransom is my turning-point; if you
Refuse it, then I warn you, any means
Are fair to me though foul to you. Do you
Understand that!

ALPHEGE. I understand more than that.

OLAF. Then, once and for all, will you understand
There is no more than that! Whatever motive
You may have, I have told you mine.

ALPHEGE. You have told me
Only what might be your motive. Good enough
So far as it goes; to reward the men you lead—
I do believe you—to restore the land
You lost, and to break the interloping tyrant.
Yes, this is good enough; but is it enough
For such as you, for such as them? Consider—

If you feel for the wrongs of suffering men—
Again I do believe you—how is this
To be accounted for, that you raise up
Reward out of the sufferings of my people,
This scene that blood has blotted, this summer land
Black with your handiwork, and the winter store
You burnt? Is suffering recompense for suffering?
No, you had not considered that, or rather
You had, and are hiding it from your heart, Olaf,
Your heart, that would not see one man degraded
Here at your feet, although a stranger.

OLAF. Well,
Say that I do this, there is no other choice.
In any case, simply to pay your ransom
Cannot degrade you.

ALPHEGE. No, but it will degrade
Your purpose, Olaf. You are to be a king!

OLAF. Do you set up to teach me that?

ALPHEGE. All teaching
Is a reminder of what we already know.
You know that if you descend the slopes of greed,
Bargain and trickery such as turned you out,
Your land were better with the Danes in charge
Than you; but when I said you were to be a king,
I meant a king like your father.

OLAF. No one names
My father to me. You are the first who has spoken
A word of him for years. What do you mean?

ALPHEGE. I mean to teach you what a king is. No,
Not altogether by him, though you do well

To remember how he was loved, and in that memory
Love him yourself. He did not buy men's lives
With blood-bought gold. He was their friend, and they
Were his. You have that in you, Olaf,
To be like him, but wiser, stronger; and more,
To make your land no longer fatherless, but
A home of souls.

OLAF. No one has spoken to me
Before like this; and least of all of him.
You can guess my first sick scraps of childhood, the shock
And the disillusion, a boy at the open window
Hearing the servants and swineherds gossip below.
But you speak to me as if this did not matter,
As if I were loosed from the lariat and the noose
Of those foredone days, as if—I do not know
How this may be—as if you were my father.

ALPHEGE. That may not be so strange. It is not I
But the Father of all you recognise through me.
Yet I could be your father; I could reach
And teach you as only a father can his son.

OLAF. What will you teach me? Can you teach it me?

ALPHEGE. If you will learn, I can teach you a better way,
The best, to reward your followers, gather your kingdom,
And be a king; and that without my ransom
Or the loss of any living soul.

OLAF. Then tell me.
I am sick, sick of playing Canute and his Danes
At their own game, and his the leopard paw
That lances out of the sleekness of his friendship
Mysterious death that steals my men; tell me

Your way to put me on my path to Norway.
I trust you as a father; tell me at once.

ALPHEGE. Here and now? Without their knowledge?

OLAF. No,
Not that either. I owe them that at least,
That is what you have taught me, not to descend
To any sleight of theirs.

ALPHEGE. That you had
Already at heart, no teaching of mine. Honour
Is what we wake with, not what we put on.
It does you honour that you will be honest
Even with them. So let me tell them all
Openly of a better reward than ransom
To seek for here. Will you do that?

OLAF. I will.
I will call them here now.

ALPHEGE. No, wait. I wish to speak
To all of you as kings, princes and leaders
In your command. I must take on myself
The outward signs of my authority here,
Enrobed in some relation to my world,
As you are to yours. Let me first go and dress
In what my title owns.

OLAF. Dress in what robes
You have; I shall still honour you as a man.
Return here to make plain my way, and give
Assurance to the rest. If you can end
The sad long Northern night of darkened youth
You shall have my allegiance, as no king
Could ever receive it; for I see in you

The rolling curtains, this aurora of blood
Sweep back to something clearer that I knew
Once, and have not quite forgotten. Father—
I call you that because your follower did—

ALPHEGE. It is what I am called; and you, my son,—
The title fits both ways. Now I shall go
To bring myself again to you, while you
Summon the others. Go in peace, my son!

[ALPHEGE *goes out in the direction of* THRYM'S *tent.*]

OLAF. In peace! Rani! Rani!

[*Enter* RANI *from the princes' tent.*]

RANI. Well, what has happened?

OLAF. Happened!

RANI. So the Archbishop has gone to fetch
The ransom, has he? Well, do we get what we asked?

OLAF. He will return to tell us of a reward
Greater than ransom.

RANI. A reward greater than ransom!
What is this? You have fixed the ransom then?
Or what is this reward?

OLAF. I do not know.

RANI. You do not!

OLAF. I am trusting him to teach me
Something you once said that you left untaught—
The way to win my kingdom. Did you not say
Often this would be so?

RANI. I did, but—this man!
It cannot be him the sign was meant for!

OLAF. Sign!
What sign?

RANI. Your mother said—it was the word
She uttered in the travail of the news
About your father—she said to me, " Rani,
Be as a father to him, until another
Even wiser shall come as a sign to him,
A sign to take his kingdom." But this Englishman—

OLAF. He is a man, Rani. He may be that one
My mother meant. I have promised us all to hear him.

RANI. And fixed no ransom! Who will tell Canute this?

OLAF. I shall. You bring Thorkel from his tent.
Tell him to keep his men and his manners in check.

RANI. But is it wise? Canute will use this. If
You want your kingdom, get this ransom now
Before they force you to share it, sail tomorrow
And quit. That is the way.

OLAF. No, not before
I know his way. You said, there will be a sign.

RANI. I learnt enough by tutoring you to plumb
The bedrock of obstinacy. Very well, do as you please.

[RANI *goes into* THORKEL'S *tent.* CANUTE *appears suddenly.*]

CANUTE. Well, have you killed the old fool?

OLAF. What? What do you mean?

CANUTE. Alphege: I warned him he would get no change
From you. Has he gone squealing for his ransom,
Or have you struck him down? I do not think
We lose much if you have.

OLAF. I do not think
You understand. He is to speak to us all
Here under my protection.

CANUTE. Speak to us!

OLAF. And
Because I have asked him.

CANUTE. Are you in some alliance?

OLAF. You wish me to explain.

CANUTE. I do.

OLAF. Then let me,
Quickly, Canute, before they come.

CANUTE. I hope
You will be able to. I hope indeed
You will. If you and I should disagree
The mountain then stands ranged against the sea.
Come in then.

[*Exeunt* OLAF *and* CANUTE *into the princes' tent, drawing the flaps.*]

The end of the First Act can be indicated here by a short interval, or by a lowering of the lights.

ACT TWO

[*Enter* STIGAND *carrying a stole,* ALPHEGE *dressed in white, with* THRYM *dodging querulously about them.*]

THRYM. I've said I'm sorry. I'll never try to strike you
Again. I see your ways are right. But all the same,
I might as well have gone to sea in a hen-coop
In mid-November for all the comfort you bring.
What is it now? There's bound to be trouble. If you
Stand up and promise them something, then give them nothing
It will be murder. Each single word you say
Pitches the people around you clean into danger.

STIGAND. None in worse danger than himself. Our peril
Is nothing to his. Be quiet.

ALPHEGE. Is this a quarrel?
Why, at this of all moments?

STIGAND. It is a quarrel
Between you and yourself, and we are helpless;
Neither I nor this man with his new-found will to serve you
Can do anything. Oh forgive us, sir, but when
We see you—

ALPHEGE. When you see me, what? Give me
My stole, if you please, my son. Well, when you see me?

STIGAND. I cannot say; but why should the Bishop send
His barge with ransom here, if it were not rightful
For you to accept it?

HRYM. Why should you risk my neck
Making me feel I must defend you, and then
Asking to be attacked?

LPHEGE. You may both leave me now
Alone, if you wish. There is no shame in your going.

HRYM. But there would be, and you know it. This
Is like a ship. Quit her to sink, you cannot,
Though every plank be stove; besides, who knows
What worse than waves if once you did!

[*Enter* OLAF *and* CANUTE, *and* RANI *and* THORKEL.]

ANUTE. So Alphege
Is here to offer a better reward than ransom!

HORKEL. At least he is punctual.

ANI. The Englishman's virtue; they have to be
Because their minds get slowly into stride.
In Latin lands they always start late, because
They know they can catch you up.

IORKEL. But once Englishmen
Make up their minds to catch time in the nick,
Much may be hoped to follow. Is that not so, Stigand?

LAF. Thorkel! Stand over there, and stop your banter.
This is serious.

IORKEL. Oh yes, indeed, most serious.

LAF. Remember it is then. Now, Alphege, we all shall judge
Whether or not there is value for us in your words.

[*The princes sit, and the hostleaders stand watching, while* HAREK *and some fightingmen appear and listen as* ALPHEGE *speaks*].

ALPHEGE. Not in my words. Words in themselves are valueless
As the tongue of a bell is useless till it strike
On metal nobly cast. To you, my sons,
Crucibled in the bronze and furnace of life,
I speak, then wait and listen, to receive
What note you give. Each of you, in his way,
Has tried to drive a bargain with me; naturally,
Since you belong to a world of bargains, of promise,
Of pain, of penalty, of praise, of reward, of ransom.
That is your world, the world to which you give
Nothing, yet expect all, to gain and get;
But you have given nothing, and therefore nothing
Will you get! The gold, the plunder, the power,
The ships, the cities, the throne itself, when you
Are dead, are nothing; for nothing of this can you keep;
No, not one single stick of the chair you sit in
Will furnish the empty freehold of death. What then
Is your adventure worth, what then the prizes
You promise to your men? Nothing. For even
If, as you say, you conquer the land and the ocean,
Hold waves and people transfixed, there still remains
A master-race that rules you. All your bodies,
Hugged over oar and rope, sweating with siege-ladder,
Six-foot axe or ram-headed battering-pole,
All your strength is outnumbered far by the bodies
Of the ever-present invisible unvanquished dead.
Not even the advantage of numbers is yours. For each man
Who helms your vessel over the grey-white sea,
A hundred bodies grit with the wake below
Waiting for his. For each man who stands on the field,
Slicing and scything the air in figures-of-eight
With gigantic axe-stroke, there lies beneath the red
Of the blood-tipped daisy a hundred sets of the bones,

The thighs and the fore-arms that hold him there. Your bodies
Exist in the candle of sun and moon, which throws
A hundred shadows behind you. Each one of these shades
Becomes your conqueror. Nothing of all your winnings,
Your gainings, your gifts, will remain when these overseers
Command you to strip and surrender.

AREK [*suddenly shouting*]. Lies! Lies! Lies!
We shall die fighting and go to feast with Odin!
All the old stories say it! It must be true! It is true!
Why do you let him say this? He is a wizard
As Thorkel said, a Lapland sorcerer, a demon—

LAF. Thorkel! Will you kennel your creature!

HORKEL [*striking* HAREK]. Stop howling!

ANUTE. I was just thinking he was not far off the scent.
Few of us here have that faith to think that we
Will see much more than dirt or sea-slime when
We die. That is no warrant to say there should be
No recompense for the living; rather more
In my opinion! Surely we were to hear
Reasons for not receiving ransom, something
Better to reward brave fellows. I myself ask
What is the benefit in this performance?

LAF. Will you
Answer Canute, Alphege?

LPHEGE. I shall answer
All of you. The treasure that does not disperse with death,
The kingdom that does not die when the prince is dead,
The bounty whose distribution contents a camp,
A race or a nation, through all generations, is here,
Here in your lives, though not as your lives now run.

It is the love of God, to love a God
Who is love itself, and in love to see the world,
The good and the beauty men may behold and do,
As a halcyon bridge of uncountable colours, each
A crystal of one pendant light, each perfect
In its own right, a pearl that cannot be shattered
In grey and trampled flakings to no purpose,
But is the true round empire universal
Creating eternal witness: such as these:—
The centuried work of scribe to scribe, immured
In monastery, yet free to paint a page
With lark's-blue heaven, and flowers, and insects, bright
With eternal tremble of ever-opening petal:—
Then too the words and wisdom not of one age
Half-remembered by the next, wholly forgotten
By grandson neglect, but adding ring to ring
Of the mid-field tree of philosophy, a great girth
Of truth growing into time: then too the gift
Of peace, not willed away by death of prince
Or change of rule, but a habit of life, a nature
Men find they are born to, just as the air they breathe,
A prize they can keep in the homestead, not scuffle and hid
Like stolen gold in cave and mountain, fearing
Reprisal for past robbery:—yes, and the power
Known to all good, to outlive all destruction—the power
Of Christ our Lord to be destroyed and yet live,
The power He has given to Canterbury to outlast
The mere defacing. This is true, and in the world,
Everywhere, and in our time, now, as we live.
And now I show you how this is, how you
May be this life, and give it as reward
Excelling ransom to all followers. Be
Servants, not rulers of each other. Be

Not men who make men die for you, but be
Those who would die for men. And if this seem hard
That one should be in pain for many, then
I tell you there is one in pain for you,
All of you, even the fiercest here; and that
Is Christ; and if you are truly His, and rule men
As His sealed servants, then I tell you now
The treasure is here. For here, look, in His sight
We are together, men and men, all one
To serve and help, not trap and put in danger
And slay, but without guile, in perfect safety,
To——

THRYM. Look out! The arrow!

[*An arrow is seen quivering in the back of* OLAF's *chair.* ALPHEGE *falls on his knees in prayer.*]

RANI. The Englishman!

THRYM. I saw him shoot it!

HAREK. After him!

[*Exeunt* THRYM, HAREK *and fightingmen.*]

CANUTE. Catch the Englishman! Remember the reward!
A bag of gold!

OLAF [*dazed*]. An English arrow!

RANI. Are you safe?
Are you unharmed? Did it strike you then?

THORKEL [*seizing* STIGAND] Here!
Swiftly! This is your moment, this is your chance,
Your only one! Quick, before the thunder! Go!

RANI. Are you unhurt? No scratch! Will you speak, Olaf!

OLAF. We were assembled to hear this Englishman speak—
And then an English arrow—

THORKEL [*to* STIGAND]. Here! Take the ring!
Now, go, go! No one will notice in the chase!
Bring back the ransom as quick as death!

[*Exit* STIGAND.]

RANI. Olaf!
Why are you clutching that arrow still? Is the barb
Caught in your flesh? Is it poisoned?

OLAF. Yes! This Englishman
Called us here to listen, our backs to danger.
Now, all in white, he kneels praying; and rightly; for now
Is his hour of death!

[*He raises the arrow with both hands.*]

THORKEL [*seizing* OLAF'*s arm*]. Stop!

OLAF [*dropping the arrow*]. You, Thorkel, you!
This is the real nightmare of day! You, Thorkel,
Protect the Archbishop!

THORKEL. I do not protect him; but wait
And do not kill him in the heat.

OLAF. You Danes
Would like to torture him! Take him, do what you like with him.
He has deceived us. Nothing would be too bad for him.
His words of love, service, and suffering—now
We know what they are worth, yes, and his God too!

RANI. Quiet, Olaf! Plunging from ice to fire
Will blister your brain!

OLAF. If you old men tell lies,
What do you expect the young to do! Canute,

Here and now I swear to make common cause
With you against all England. We'll set a torch
To every house and farm; in every church
We'll nail them up to burn. Then when no Englishman
Is left alive, we'll raise our feast-halls here
In the ruins, and drink and drink to the old true gods.
Choose to do this, Canute, and I shall be
Your follower!

RANI. Make no hasty promises, Olaf.
Remember your kingdom.

OLAF. My kingdom is revenge,
My promise, hate. Take my allegiance, Canute!

[CANUTE, *who has remained seated, stands up triumphant. Enter* HAREK, *howling and crying, who falls at his feet.*]

HAREK. Canute! Canute! Justice! Justice! Justice!

CANUTE. Harek! What is this!

HAREK. Justice! I ask for justice!

THORKEL. Get up, man! What is it? Get up!

HAREK. No, no, I will not.
I will hold your chair till you give me justice, Canute,
Justice, Danish justice!

CANUTE. I will give you justice.
Now, stop slavering like a bullock. Wipe
Your slimy muzzle and tell us what is the matter.

HAREK. The matter? I have been robbed by the Norsemen.

RANI. Robbed!

HAREK. Yes, robbed! I saw the Englishman as he ran
Out of our camp. He darted away from the river
Up the hill like a deer with leaps and bounds
Over the hummocky grass; but I ran faster
Than all our men; I gained, uphill though it was,
I came to his heels, I leapt for the nape of his neck
Plump in my grasp, when out of the earth, it seemed,
Like a bear or a beast that had lain there, something hooped up
Its back and struck me full in the belly and sent me
Headlong, a bag without breath, and my head on the stone,
And the Englishman gone, gone, just as I gripped him.

CANUTE. You lost him!
He has escaped!

HAREK. Wait, wait! Listen to this!
When the mist cleared out of my skull and I picked myself up
In the heath, what should I find that the others had seized
But a woman!

THORKEL. A woman shot that arrow!

HAREK. No,
A woman tripped me, saved the man that shot it
Just as I caught him. Canute, make good your word,
Give me the reward! Give me the bag of gold!
Give it to me!

CANUTE. The bag of gold was for him
Who brought the right hand of the rebel. Have you brought it?

HAREK. No, but in my own hand I had him, I had—

CANUTE. And now
You have him not. You let him slip through your fingers.
The right man to reward!

RANI. And who are you
To say the Norsemen robbed you, you dolt? Your own idiocy
Has done it.

HAREK. No, they have. It is Thrym who has got
The woman. Give her to me for my revenge.
She at least is mine.

[*Enter* THRYM, WOMAN, *and others.*]

There! There is the woman!

WOMAN. And there is the man! The man! Yes, him! I heard you
Howling and blubbering like a brute monster. You,
A man! And you, and you! You are beasts, cattle,
Nothing else!

THRYM [*holding her*]. Stop this! You will make it worse for yourself!

WOMAN. Worse! What could be worse than have these animals
Trampling our land! I spit at them! Now do
Your worst, and worse than worst.

THORKEL. What have you caught?

THRYM. Something with too many claws in it. Will you stay still
now!

HAREK. Give her to me. I shall teach her.

CANUTE. Wait one moment.
This teaches us, I think, how much to trust
These English of all sorts. You see, Olaf,
These are the people your loving-kindness Archbishop
Leads, and would have us at peace with, and leave to be
The savages that they are. Look at him praying!
What brutal scheming wriggles like an adder
Out of that silver nest!

WOMAN [*trying to reach him*]. O my lord Archbishop!
Oh it is you! Oh forgive me, forgive me!

THRYM [*restraining her*]. Come here!
Be quiet!

CANUTE. You see, Olaf, no trusting these people
Whatever their condition.

WOMAN. No, that is not true.
We are what we are because you have made us. We
Were not like this before you came. [*to* ALPHEGE] O my lord—

CANUTE. He is not your lord. He is only an old man deserving
Of death. We are the lords of you and your land.

WOMAN [*breaks free and kneels to* OLAF].
You! And none of you human! Yes, but there is one!
That one there, the silent one! There is hope there!
There, in his face, there is light, there is hope. Yes,
You, you will see justice done to me!

HAREK. What!
Some plot of the Norsemen again! Give her up! Give her up!

OLAF. Silence! There are webs I cannot push from my mind
As if this were a dream; but if one of you comes
Within an arm's length, I shall try on his skull
Whether I am dreaming. It seems I am asked for justice.
Is it the law of Norway this woman demands?

CANUTE. If you dream rightly, you may remember you swore
Norway to us.

RANI. He did not. This interrupted him.
I say this is a sign!

OLAF. [*turning to where* ALPHEGE *still kneels*]. A sign!

HAREK. She is mine!

OLAF. I think Thrym captured her. I think, sign or no sign,
She is ours, within our law, and free to ask
To be judged by us, not you.

CANUTE. To be judged by you!
When an arrow from one of her people nearly killed you?
You must be mad, or even more of a child
Than I had thought. Why, cut her throat or throw her
To your fightingmen, but stop this infant drool
Of justice dribbling down your chin!

OLAF. She asked
For justice. I am the heir of Norway, and
No child. She came as a sign. She shall be judged.

CANUTE. Gods give me patience with you, Olaf! Do you
Intend to be her advocate before us—
You who abuse us if we lay a finger
On one of your Norsemen, now come forward as
The protector of the murderer of your men!
Look, she lies weeping at your feet. What case,
What judgment can there be, when she cannot speak
Except to confess a crime we already know?
What person here would plead for her?

[ALPHEGE *has risen to his feet unnoticed.*]

ALPHEGE. I would.
That is the reason I am still here. I am here
To plead for this woman, as I should indeed.
She is not guilty. I am the one who is guilty!

OLAF. Guilty! You! Then this was a conspiracy!
You brought us here to kill us!

[*He advances again on* ALPHEGE, *but the* WOMAN *leaps to her feet.*]

WOMAN. No, no, he did not!
[*to* ALPHEGE] Oh no, my lord, no, no! You knew nothing,
Nothing of this! [*to the rest*] My husband shot that arrow,
Yes, that and others before. And I wish I saw them
Now, sticking in some of your gullets. That would
Teach you to slash your accusations about
Like idiot schoolboys switching the heads off flowers
On the way to school. We mean to teach you something!
But the lord Archbishop knows nothing of this. All England
Knows he is here; but he is altogether innocent.

CANUTE. Then why does he say he is guilty?

ALPHEGE. Because I am guilty.

WOMAN. No, no, my lord—

ALPHEGE. My daughter! Let me speak.
A man kneeling in prayer may live a life
While a star falls or a bird's wing passes. I
Have lived that life. I stand in front of you all
A different man from my five-minute-ago
Self, which spoke up so confidently, so wrongly.

OLAF. Was nothing true you said to us?

ALPHEGE. It was
All true, but not as it came from me. I am
Guilty of the worst fault of those who work
For peace, the fault of those who speak and preach
Without the deed, who say and do not do.
They are the makers of violence. They will make
More war than the war-makers, till at last they learn

Not passively to stand and be right, but to be
Something more great and giving than in the right,
Something that does not goad the rest to acts
That shudder at themselves.

OLAF. As you have goaded me
Almost to swear away my life and my kingdom.

ALPHEGE. That is my guilt.

CANUTE. And how do you propose to amend it?

ALPHEGE. By what I shall do.

HAREK. The flap-hooded ravens of Odin
Peck out your eyes, you old stumbling shuffling wizard!
Give up that woman.

ALPHEGE. I shall defend this woman.
That is what I demand to do.

CANUTE. Demand!

ALPHEGE. Yes, demand; and from you, Olaf.

OLAF. Very well.
Defend this woman; and be yourself on trial!

HAREK. No, no, no!

THRYM. Yes; she is in our justice,
Not in your jaws yet.

THORKEL. Someone had better accuse her.
We must have justice all round.

RANI. It seems we have,
Especially with Thorkel taking a latter-day interest
In law and order. Well, then, who does accuse her?
This boar with foam on his tusks?

HAREK. Help me, Canute,
Help, as you promised. You see the Norsemen stand
On the side of the sorcerer.

CANUTE. Yes, I do; and that
Is enough accusation. I do not need to accuse
The woman. She has accused herself. Nor does it
Account whether she and this Englishman are in conspiracy.
Their hearts keep step to do us harm; but this
Is my real accusation, that he has ranged the Norsemen
Now, as you see, against us; that by his words
As much as arrows, he means to drive a bolt
Of discord in our flesh, and split our camp
Like a marksman's wand. He means to do this, and
This will mean murder, of a sort.

OLAF. Will you
Answer this accusation, Alphege?

ALPHEGE. I shall,
But under English law; and by that law
You must not name us guilty before trial,
Nor is plain accusation and denial
The course, the black affirmation set against
The white response. Truth is an object of question,
And I shall question this woman.

OLAF. Very well; do so.

CANUTE. And question yourself; the finger is pointing to you.

ALPHEGE. So be it. Come here, my daughter. No one will hurt you
If you answer me truly. Now, what is your husband's name?

WOMAN. Aldwyn of Greenwich, and a good man.

ALPHEGE. Where do you live?

Safe on the wharf, ready to come on board.
Now will you let him go?

ALPHEGE. My son, my son,
What have you done?

THORKEL [*to* STIGAND]. Why, what any brave fellow would!
I think you have something of mine?

STIGAND. Take back your ring!

THORKEL. Why, it is not poisoned.

STIGAND. I do not know. Look at him.
Oh, what have I done?

THORKEL [*to* ALPHEGE]. Stupefied by good fortune?
You have friends, you see, in little-looked-for places.
Alphege, you have friends.

ALPHEGE. Friends who help me to this!

THORKEL. Yes, and they mean you to use it.

ALPHEGE. And so I shall.
Here, Canute. Here is your money for this woman.

WOMAN. Oh no, my lord, no.

STIGAND. Oh father, what are you doing?
Who is this woman?

ALPHEGE. No less than I am.

THORKEL. And you
Are nothing less than a madman. Take back the money!
Use it for yourself!

[*He snatches it from* CANUTE *and thrusts it back to* ALPHEGE.]

ALPHEGE. I have the right to use it
For whom I please. Have I not that right, Canute?

CANUTE. You had better ask Olaf. He is your partner in this.

ALPHEGE. Olaf?

[OLAF *takes the bag and throws it down in front of* HAREK.]

OLAF. Pick up your reward then, Harek the Dane!

THRYM. What are you waiting for, Harek? Are you afraid?

HAREK. No one ever refused sound money; but I tell you
There will be something to settle later.

[*He picks it up.*]

OLAF. It is settled
Now. She is free.

CANUTE. And Alphege? The rest of the ransom
That even his friends are willing to offer and fetch,
Do we see nothing of that? Or are we to prove
The truth of his words, that he is willing to die?—
This spider with his threading together of lies,
Curdling friendship with his cuckoo-spit venom
Into enmity, who cannot see the truth for—

OLAF. Who sees you, Canute, and farther than you, as I
Do now. He is still in the circuit of our law.
Rani, guard the woman out of the camp!
Thrym, keep your axe-head raised beside them! Put her
Safely into the hands of her friends.

WOMAN [*to* ALPHEGE]. My lord,
What shall I say?

ALPHEGE. Say nothing. Give thanks to God.
Let all understand that whatever there is to come,
There must be no revenge. And so bless you, my daughter.

RANI. Come quickly! Thrym!

[*Exeunt* RANI, THRYM, *and* WOMAN.]

OLAF. And now hear what I say!
I say this man has proved his words, not lies
But truth out of range of your spittle of hate. I say
He shall be out of range of your revenge.
Since he will not be ransomed, I renounce
His ransom, and all claim upon it.

DANES. No, no!

OLAF. Silence!
Listen! My tent is now his home and sanctuary.
I here forbid, on pain of death from me
At my own hands, that any weapon of any sort
Be raised against the Archbishop. This is an oath
Binding on each man here, by whatsoever
God he believes.

HAREK. And what if we do not care
To obey such an oath!

OLAF [*striking him down*]. Let no one look for life
One minute later than disobedience! Now go,
Go and let this be known in every corner
And rat-hole of our common camp. Let it be known
For truth!

[*Exeunt* HAREK *and Danish and Norse fightingmen.*]

Alphege, what princedom I have is yours
For a short stay here; but, short as it is, I need you

Here at this moment of my life. And yet
You are free to go at once. I would not keep you
In such company as I have kept.

CANUTE. Well, Olaf.
This is a quick turn-round with your oldest friends.
Never mind. Thorkel, since I am exiled from
My tent of command, I will borrow yours. You have
A chessboard too. It suits me perhaps to play
A game on yours.

THORKEL. If it relieves your mind
You are very welcome.

CANUTE. It may relieve my mind
Indeed. Thank you, Thorkel.

[*Exeunt* CANUTE *with* THORKEL *into his tent.*]

OLAF. And you, Alphege,
Will you go now to your friends on the river, or trust
My help, and lend me yours? I stand alone
On a thawing icefloe of purpose, which bears down
Over such falls as I cannot guess, though I hear
The crack and snarl of decision ahead. Will you
Stay beside me or go?

ALPHEGE. Stigand, you brought
The expectation of our friends beyond
This camp. They wait to see me, I suppose.

STIGAND. They do, they do, each one praying that you
Will soon be with them safe; but I—

ALPHEGE. What do
You say now, Stigand? You have seen our universe
Visibly alter in these environs. Have you
Found alteration with it?

STIGAND. Yes, I have.
Oh father, not that I feel you one inch less
In danger; but I have seen the danger of
This world to be the cheat it is, the ghost
Whose turnip glare destroys the ignorant
And credulous, but which the wise man knows for
The simulacrum of nothing. So now I say
That if you know it is right to stay, then stay
And forgive our doubting selves.

ALPHEGE. And forgive myself
All too-great certainty. Will you then say this
To all who wait for me? And say again
There must be no revenge.

STIGAND. I shall return
Within a moment of persuading them.
You must not remain alone.

[*Exit* STIGAND.]

ALPHEGE. Truly I shall not.
You see, Olaf, I am staying with you.

OLAF. I see
You are as good as your word. I see now how
It was with Thrym. But what should I do? Tell me
What I do now.

ALPHEGE. You do rightly all that
You would have done wrongly. Give up this strained alliance
Of seeming-good. Leave England. Lead off your men,
Not with a golden halter round their neck
And yours, but to the founding of God's kingdom
In your inheritance, not bought with blood and burning
And the whip-drive of brutality, but as a servant

Of God and your people. Do this in Norway, or
Whatever name men give to God's estate
Of earth, and you will hold your kingdom.

OLAF. And will
You come and help me to do this? Come and be
A father to me and my country?

ALPHEGE. No, Olaf, not I.
You must do this alone; and yet not alone,
Being alone with God, as we were at our birth
And will be at our death.

OLAF. Then tell me one thing.
Did you come as a sign, as my mother said,
Or was this only an accident, such a chance
As sometimes may save one man on a broken sea
And crush another to a barrel-hoop? Is all our life
The hap and hazard of a chance?

ALPHEGE. It is no chance.
Our natures are not chance, though chance may mark
Those natures. Do not wonder. The soul's language
Is written in slow script. Let me now show you
How this may be. Those few effects you brought
From Canterbury with contempt, the silver, the gold,
The goblets, the cross, the candlesticks, yes, I have seen them
Kicked like refuse in the corner of your tent—those things
Are poor, as you say, in themselves; but they are pointers
To a rich mystery. Let me teach you here
Under the canvas of your command to value
These instruments of service, and set up
God's altar in the judging-place of death.
Come, let me show you.

[*He moves toward the princes' tent as* STIGAND *re-enters.*]

STIGAND. Father!

OLAF. What is it?

ALPHEGE. Stigand!
You are back soon.

STIGAND. I have not been able to go.

OLAF. Why not?

STIGAND. Danes, at the camp-gate, drinking and buying
Drink. They would not let me pass.

OLAF. They would not?
They will! These Danes even now! Come with me! Alphege,
Be free of my tent till I return to see
Your mystery.

ALPHEGE. I shall be here when you return.
I shall be here.

OLAF. Keep at my heel, Stigand.
These Danes!

[*Exeunt* OLAF *and* STIGAND.]

ALPHEGE. I shall be here.

[*He goes into the princes' tent, closing the flaps.* THORKEL *staggers from his own tent, followed by* CANUTE.]

THORKEL. No, no, not murder!
Anything but murder!

CANUTE. He could have had
His life a hundred times.

THORKEL. Say what you like. I will not
Be the man to do it.

CANUTE. No? And why? Because
You, Thorkel, are the one who thinks himself
The man to come clean-handed to every party,
The popular man among men; but you are not,
My friend, nor ever will be.

THORKEL. Canute, I had no—

CANUTE. Such thoughts! I read you, Thorkel, as the pilot
Reads the sea-chart. I know every shelf
And bank which you keep hidden. You rule England!
Not in my lifetime, Thorkel—still less in yours.

THORKEL. Very well. Say my life is short. I will not
Spatter its ending with your blood-letting. You
Have years to live this down. Do your own work!

CANUTE. I do; and a greater work than you; so you
Must be my scavenger. You know, Thorkel, my father
Expects a good report of you. I write
Reports in blood.

THORKEL. Why? Why not let him go?

CANUTE. He mouses in the store-room of my plan,
He and Olaf.

THORKEL. He and Olaf! And Olaf
Protects him in that tent. Have you thought of that?

CANUTE. If Olaf puts an arm out between destruction
And the Archbishop—well, you are a tall man,
Thorkel, and broad. Your shoulders are broad enough
To bear two corpses.

THORKEL. No!

CANUTE. Yes, if need be!
But choose your way to do it. You need not
Be there yourself. Indeed, if you and I
Were in company in your tent, it would be better;
But make it certain!

THORKEL. If there were a way to be certain!—
But we promised not even to raise a weapon.

CANUTE. Promises,
Thorkel, are patterns to re-arrange; and so
Are men. You said yourself you could rule men.

[HAREK *staggers in with a drinking-horn and a wine-skin.*]

HAREK. Gold! Gold! Gold and bones!

[*He sprawls across a table among the ox-bones.*]

CANUTE. As perhaps this man.

THORKEL. Go into my tent, Canute! Set out the chess-board!
I shall be with you.

CANUTE. I see, Thorkel.

[*He goes into the tent.*]

HAREK. Gold!
Too much gold! And the wine not blood. The bones
All white and empty, no blood!

THORKEL. Harek!

HAREK. Thorkel!
That's a good joke. Thorkel protects the Archbishop.
Take the Archbishop's gold, Thorkel. There's much
Too much of it! I threw it at the old woman
Selling wine at the gate. I threw it all over

The others until they grinned and jumped like dogs!
There's still too much, and the bones stare through the wine.
Why did he say our bodies would all be bones,
Bones without blood? Why did he say no feasting
When we were dead? Take back his gold, Thorkel,
Thorkel, his friend!

THORKEL. Suppose I were not his friend?

HAREK. Suppose—! Thorkel takes care to be friends
With everybody. We say he only hits you
To show how much he loves you. Thorkel likes
To think we love him too. We love you because
You're strong, Thorkel. Lop off your head, we couldn't
Care less.

THORKEL. Never mind that. You hate the Archbishop.
He cheated you.

HAREK. Take back his gold and tell him
I hope it kills him.

THORKEL. I will; but why not you
Kill him yourself?

HAREK. Oh no, oh no! Then Olaf
Kills me, and I shall be only bones. You heard
The oath—no weapon. [*Drinks.*] Ha! It would be strange
To kill him with these bones.

THORKEL. The bones!

HAREK [*playing with the ox-bones on the table*]. Litter
And clutter of feast, great ox-bones—no one believes
We shall be only bones! No! No! No!

THORKEL. No!
Nor you shall be. Listen. He is a wizard

In there. You heard me say so. Kill the old man
And your fears in one.

HAREK. He is protected.

THORKEL. " Raise
No weapon," Olaf said. You said, these bones—
No sword, no spear, no axe, no arrow, but bones!
No weapon, Harek!

HAREK. No weapon! Bones!

THORKEL. Drink! [*they drink*].

HAREK [*cautious*]. Is this certain? No punishment?

THORKEL. Olaf
Chose his own words; and if he should try to stop you—

HAREK. These bones, their death-feast! I'll call the rest.
I must have hands to help. [*calling*] Haro! Haro!
Haro! To me, Danes!

THORKEL. Quiet, quiet!

HAREK. They're coming.
Where are you going?

THORKEL. I shall be in my tent.

HAREK. You swear, no punishment.

THORKEL. Call on Thorkel, if any
Should raise an arm. Remember, they are not weapons!
Remember, it was your own idea.

[THORKEL *goes into his tent.* HAREK *sits playing with the bones.*]

HAREK. My idea!

[*Two or three Danish fightingmen come in drunk.*]

Hear Harek, his idea! And quiet now, quiet!
Not a word from a dog's throat of you! You've had my gold,
You've had my wine. Now listen what deeds deserve it.
There's an old wizard who plots the end of the world
In there, behind Olaf's tent-flap. The end of the world!
The great end that it should be, the heroes' end!
Hear Harek's voice, listen to no more lies.
Hear me! We are the heroes, the Danes; the Norse
Nothing, the English empty, all except craft
And cunning. We are the heroes. Drink! Drink!
To the world's end!

[*They drink.*]

Look now! Scarlet and gold
The red-wattled chanticleer crows at evening. The clouds
Swarm at the throat of the gasping sun. They have him,
They have him, the grey jaws have him! Now crevicing
Out of their caverns the underworld people slime
And coil, dwarfs with lop-nodding heads, mountains
With legs like children, women with breasts like pigs—
Only the heroes are clean. Stand upright! Drink, drink,
The heroes! Drink to the world's end!

[*They drink.*]

Fury and blood
Lie on the land. The gods and giants are fighting,
Axe and thunderstone, mist, blood on the battlefield,
Blood, to the knee, to the hip, to the heart, to the head.
Drink, drink to the world's end!

[*They drink.*]

We shall be free, the heroes!
And the dwarfs and the wizards, the snakes in their covins
Be crushed beneath bones and blood. Take up these ox-bones!

The blood of the ox on each brow! Now swear, swear,
Swear by the raising of bones to blood these bones
On the wizard within that tent. This oath answers
The other. These are not weapons. I will lead you,
Heroes, to the world's end! Drink!

DANES. Drink! To the world's end!

HAREK. Lift up these bones and give these bones blood! The gods
Fight with us. They call for blood. Look, look, the raven!
The raven hangs over the tent, croaking, choking for blood!
Blood, let the bones taste blood, the blood of the wizard,
The blood of the dragon of lies! Blood, blood, blood!

[*They tear open the princes' tent, hurling on one side the chairs of justice as they do.* ALPHEGE *is praying before an altar on which the candles are lit. They pause and draw back for a moment. He raises his hands in prayer.*]

DANES. Blood!

[*They dash the bones down on him as* OLAF, RANI *and* THRYM *enter.*]

OLAF. What is this!

HAREK. No weapon, Olaf, no weapon!
Bones, only bones, bones, bones, blood and bones!

[*The murderers, grouped round the tent, throw the blood-stained bones down on the ground in front of them.*]

OLAF. Murderer!

HAREK [*retreating*]. No, no, no weapon! Thorkel! Thorkel!

OLAF. Thorkel!
You first, you first then—

ALPHEGE [*very feebly*]. No revenge! No revenge, Olaf!

OLAF. What! Alive! Out of the way!

[*He dashes into the tent, then comes back slowly.*]

RANI. Is he still alive?

OLAF. A thread, so thin, so stretched, so frail, that mercy—
Thrym! Your axe, and finish.

THRYM. No, no, Olaf!
Not him!

OLAF. Take your axe, Thrym, in mercy.

THRYM [*shows cross*]. No!
I cannot. I cannot, I tell you. I am one of his men.
Kill me if you like. I cannot kill him. I am his.

OLAF. I am his too, Thrym. Yes, Thrym, I am his;
And I say, take your axe, Thrym; in mercy, Thrym,
In mercy.

[THRYM *goes slowly behind the others. The axe rises and falls He shuts the tent-flap, comes back, and throws the axe down among the pile of bones on the ground.*]

HAREK. The weapon! Guilty! Your own words, Olaf!
The Norsemen, the Norsemen are guilty!

OLAF. I will show you
Who is guilty.

[OLAF *goes across to* THORKEL'S *tent, and throws it open* THORKEL *and* CANUTE *are playing chess.*]

CANUTE. And check! Olaf!

OLAF. Canute.
The game is over.

THORKEL. Over?

OLAF. And Thorkel. Come out.
No, no one will harm you. The harm is done.
Yet his poor candle-flame has salved the bite
Of your dog's tooth. There will be no revenge.

CANUTE. Olaf, you may not believe me—

OLAF. I know now
What to believe. I believe he was a sign
Sent to me here.

RANI. Olaf!

OLAF. Yes, Rani, wisdom
Can often be right without knowledge. As you wanted,
We are leaving England.

CANUTE. And our alliance, Olaf?
Not for this world will you dare to break our alliance.

OLAF. I break my alliance with you, Canute, as you
And your kindred have broken alliance with humankind.

THORKEL. We hear the guilt of this murder was yours.

OLAF. You do,
Thorkel, and you could never be wrong; but right
Or wrong, payment or debt, Norseman or Dane,
This man's death is a lodestone of life that turns me
True and away from you.

CANUTE. He intends to desert us!

OLAF. I intend to be as man was intended. Canute,
You know what little is left to say. Call off
Your men to the farthest circuit of our camp,

Away out of here. Let no last-minute violence
Hurry the deliberate haste of our departure,
Or that unknown whose hand is here may take
A deadlier part.

CANUTE. Withdraw our people, Thorkel.

[*Exeunt* THORKEL, HAREK, *and the Danish fightingmen.*]

OLAF. Now, at the last, will you shake hands, Canute?

CANUTE. I think, Olaf, you are shaking hands with death.
Find out your kingdom where you like, and I
Will find you, Olaf. My great ocean will
Submerge your mountains, and your corpse will come
Floating stiff to my feet. Well, Olaf, till then!

[*Exit* CANUTE.]

OLAF [*restraining* RANI]. Let him go!

RANI. And where do we go?

OLAF. I go
To find my kingdom and rule it, my own kingdom,
Not cap-in-hand with promise and reward
And power, but in the vulnerable strength
Of peace. Trust me, Rani, to have learnt
A lesson even equal the life it has cost.

[*Enter* STIGAND.]

STIGAND. I heard—

OLAF. You have heard nothing that was not true.

[STIGAND *kneels.*]

And yet you have not heard the hundredth part
Of what is still to perform. Stay here and watch.
We go to warp his funeral barge ashore,

Then he up the river home, and we away
To sea, departure that is new beginning
For both. If you can bear to look upon
The answer to the world's question, it is here.

[*Exeunt* OLAF, RANI, *and* THRYM. STIGAND *slowly stands up.*]

STIGAND. It is here. What is this life whose secret is
So plain, and yet eludes us? What is this death
We bring upon the best that life provides?
Give me and every man a thousand years
To search, and we shall still wander. Father, I come.

[*He crosses himself, then draws himself up, and enters the tent, closing the flaps behind him. The stage is completely empty as the play ends.*]